The Fifth Taste of human being

UMAMI
THE WORLD

Contents

65   Basic Information about Umami

Umami: A Universal Taste The World Over

Introduction

Eastern discovers versus Western

Introduction

The flavor of food is determined by a number of different factors including taste, smell, color, temperature and overall appearance, as well as by physiological or psychological conditions. The most important factors are the basic tastes of sweet, sour, salty, bitter and umami. Although there is no English word for it, umami is a savory taste imparted by glutamate and 5 ribonucleotides, including inosinate and guanylate, which occur naturally in many foods including meat, fish, vegetables and dairy products. The taste of umami itself is subtle. It blends well with other tastes to expand and round out flavors. Most people don't recognize umami when they encounter it, but it can be detected when eating tomatoes, Parmesan cheese, cured ham, mushrooms, sun-dried tomatoes, meat and fish, etc.

Who first identified the taste of glutamate?

Almost 100 years ago, a Japanese scientist, Prof. Kikunae Ikeda, recognized a common factor in the complicated flavors of asparagus, tomatoes, cheese and meat, which was quite distinctive and could not be classified under any of the well defined taste qualities: sweet, sour, salty and bitter. He started investigating the main taste substance of dried seaweed (kombu), because he could detect it most clearly in soup stock prepared with kombu. Soup stock or 'dashi', in Japanese has been traditionally used in Japanese cuisine for more than 1000 years. He discovered that the taste was produced by glutamate contained in dried kombu, and named it 'umami'. After the discovery of umami, Ikeda tried to develop a new flavoring substance based on glutamate, compatible with the natural taste of foods. Finally he found that monosodium glutamate (MSG) was the best flavoring because it was readily soluble in water, had a strong umami taste, high stability, and absorbed no humidity. MSG was first marketed in Japan in 1909. His discovery of umami, along with the introduction of the new seasoning, MSG, made an important contribution to the food industry. His idea of using glutamate, which is one of the amino acids (building blocks of protein), in seasoning, was the world's first product based on a single amino acid. The Japanese Government Patent Office have listed Prof. Ikeda as one of the ten greatest Japanese inventors. (http://www.jpo.go.jp/indexj.htm).

Eastern discoveries versus Western

Bouillon has traditionally been used in western countries. Bouillon cubes were first commercially made by the Swiss flour manufacturer, Julius Magi, in 1882. He developed and produced them for people who could not afford meat, as an inexpensive method of making nutritious soup. Rapid-cooking dehydrated soups evolved into an important business segment in western countries. A meaty flavor from hydrolyzed plant protein was an indispensable factor used to satisfy Western people. At that time, it was not known that this taste was mainly imparted by glutamate, which is most abundant in protein hydrolysates. Two discoveries; the bouillon cube in the West and MSG in the East, reflect traditional dietary culture in Europe and Japan. The taste of bouillon is made up of various components contained in meat and vegetables. The taste of 'dashi' is mainly made up of glutamate from dried kombu or nucleotides from dried bonito. The most important taste element in both bouillon and dashi is umami, imparted by glutamate or nucleotides. Although the traditional way of enriching taste in various dishes in Europe and Japan differs, the key component in the bouillon cube and MSG is the same; umami by glutamate.

As a Japanese scientist first discovered umami, many people believe it to be a uniquely oriental taste element, but in fact it has existed traditionally not only in Eastern, but also Western culture. The story of 'Umami in Western Cuisine' by Elizabeth Rozin starting on page 28 will give you a new insight into the taste.

Umami in Asian Countries

Fermented products in Southeast Asia

Chinese cuisine and umami

Traditional Japanese cuisine
- Kombu
- Dried bonito (katsuobushi)
- Dashi, the most simple umami soup
- Soy sauce

Culinary art and science

Umami rich ingredients have been valued not only for their taste but also for their ability to enhance and bring out the original flavor of food. Fermented fish sauce and paste made from fish or small shrimps and fermented bean products, have long been used in Asian countries.

If you take a look at a map showing areas where rice was cultivated in the 15th century, you will see that rice was cultivated in most of the Asian countries. Rice is an important food material, used to sustain the large populations of Asian countries. As the protein in rice is better quality than that of wheat, rice is eaten as a source of protein as well as carbohydrate,

while people in Western countries keep a nutritional balance by eating meat, poultry and dairy products as a protein source, and wheat or potatoes as carbohydrates. In Asian countries, people eat a variety of nutritionally balanced fermented food with plain steamed rice, or as a rich accompaniment to cooked rice. The combination of salt and umami is a very important taste component which provides a fantastic harmony of tastes when eaten with rice.

Fermented products in Southeast Asia

There are a wide variety of different fermented products in Asian countries, e.g. Num Pla in Thailand, Nuoc Mum in Vietnam, Terasi in Indonesia, Ngapi in Burma, Pagoon in the Philippines, etc. All of these products are made by fermenting fish or shrimps. Prof. Ishige, a Japanese dietary histologist, conducted a large-scale survey on around three hundred different kinds of fermented fish and shrimp products in 13 Asian countries in the early 1980's. He reported that fermented products in Asian countries are usually used like salt or seasonings in western countries. Fermented fish or shrimp products are made by first adding large amounts of salt to fresh fish or shrimps and then keeping them under natural sunshine for at least three months. The natural protein in them decomposes into various amino acids. These amino acids and salt are important taste substances in these fermented products. Analyses of the amino acid content in fermented products show that glutamate is the most abundant amino acid. A comparison between taste components of fish sauce and soy sauce shows that salt in fish sauce, at 26%, is higher than that of soy sauce, at 17%, while the amino acid content in fish and soy sauces is almost the same, 5%. Out of the twenty kinds of different amino acids found in both sauces, Glutamate, the most abundant amino acid, is around 0.8% in both sauces. Thus the biggest difference between fish and soy sauce is the salt content. Fish sauces simply add a salty and umami taste to dishes. In Southeast Asian countries, fish sauces are used like seasoning.

There are different grades of fish sauce. Prof. Ishige showed that the grade of fish sauce, namely the cost of the fish sauce, depended on the glutamate content. The most expensive sauce, the 'first grade', has the highest content of glutamate. The higher the grade, the more glutamate the sauce contains. From their long experience in the use of fish sauces in cooking, people in Southeast Asian countries have realized that umami and salt are important taste enhancers.

Chinese cuisine and umami

In Chinese cuisine, umami in soup stock has been skillfully used for subtle harmony in various dishes. In the sixth century, Jia Sixie provided a recipe for clear soup in his book, ' The Essentials of Household Practices' (Qimin Yaoshu). To prepare stock, take the bones of a cow or sheep, crush into small pieces and simmer for a long time. To obtain a clear soup, skim off the scum rising to the top. This is the oldest recorded recipe for preparing clear stock or 'qing-tang' in Chinese. The stock-producing practice today is virtually unchanged as the Chinese still use the bones of their livestock, which are crushed into pieces and boiled for a long time. This soup is used to season food and to produce the hallmark of Chinese cuisine.

The top quality soups are known as 'shang-tang' or 'gao-tang'. Other types of soup include 'er-tang' or second-stock soup, and 'nai-tang' (a cloudy white soup with a thick taste). Soup preparation is one of the most important kitchen tasks in restaurants as it is the basic step in creating the umami taste of Chinese food. How crucial the soup is becomes clear when we consider that the 'swallow's nest' and the 'shark fin' have no taste of their own. The taste comes about as a result of the combination of ingredients, producing a very delicate swallow's nest and shark fin soup. A hotel chef explains that I kin (1.32 lbs) of soup can be made from I kin of ingredients. The cloudy white thick soup called nai-tang is prepared from chicken bones and stringy pork boiled with the addition of meat from an old chicken. Again the pound per pound rule applies, in other words, I kin of ingredients produces I kin of soup of the finest grade. It takes a long time to prepare a good stock soup, and the stock is used not only for making soups but also as a kind of seasoning adding a rich flavor and harmony of taste to various dishes.

Let us compare the Chinese stock with its Japanese equivalent. The almost instant way in which the stock is obtained from seaweed (kombu) and bonito flakes in Japan contrasts with the time-consuming Chinese boiling and simmering process. The fundamental difference is that Japanese food prefers a pure taste whereas Chinese cuisine favors a fuller, subtle blend of tastes. This may be due to the difference in the quality of Japanese and Chinese water. China has hard water with a high mineral content. Sometimes it may even have an odd taste or smell. To make a soup, it is therefore best to simmer the ingredients. In the pursuit of delicious taste, Chinese cuisine prefers an indefinable blend of a variety of tastes. This is true of Chinese soups and teas, which are part of the

Chinese eating culture. Again, this preference may be due to the Chinese way of life in which water itself cannot offer a delicious taste of its own.

Chinese cuisine makes use of a wide range of fermented products that have had a long tradition. They also give an umami taste as well as soup stock. 'Douchi' and 'chi', the fermented black foods based on soya, are semi-dried granular condiments. The mortal remains of a female believed to be the royal consort of a regional ruler, and the copious variety of burial gifts unearthed in the Maoutaikanbo (ancient tomb) excavation in Hunan, Changsha, caused a sensation throughout the world. The archeological find considered by experts to go back to the second century B.C., included some food items, among them 14g of douchi-jiang (a ginger-added douchi). The fact that this douchi dated back over 2000 years, underscores

how old this condiment is. Douchi can be eaten on its own and is also commonly used in small chunks as a food seasoning with herbal tastes such as garlic.

In East Asia and Southeast Asia, fish sauces, soybean paste (miso) and soy sauces are indispensable materials in the kitchen.

Jiang, made from grain crops, is also a very important fermented condiment in China. Based on historical records, ancient jiang were mostly made from meat and fish. They were prepared by pickling finely chopped meat or fish with salt and yeast in a sealed jar. The food was eaten with the jiang flavor by selecting the one best suited to a particular style of cooking. The jiang prepared from grain was well-known in the first century B.C. The type of jiang used today is bean paste. There are three types of bean paste; 'Huang jean', 'Tianmian-jiang', and 'Douban-jiang'. The second and third are the famous jiang used for Peking duck and Sichuan cuisine. Soy sauce and fish sauce (Yulu) and many other fermented products are widely used in Chinese cuisine. All of the items are salt-based condiments. They generate the umami and salty tastes, imparting a complex gustatory spectrum acquired in the fermentation process.

As mentioned above, various types of fermented products have been traditionally used in Eastern countries. They are all rich in umami and salty tastes. There is an interesting report stating that sauces made in the UK are composed of 32% salt, 19% processed food and 11% dairy food, while Japanese sauces are composed of 13% salt, 27% soy sauce and 16% miso. This data suggests that Asian people have traditionally been using their unique fermented seasoning to add salty and umami tastes to their dishes.

Traditional Japanese cuisine

In Japan, 'dashi' is an important material, just like all-purpose soup stock that is usually made from kombu (dried seaweed), katsuobushi (dried bonito) and dried shiitake mushroom. Dashi, literally meaning 'boiled extract' has a very simple umami taste compared with the taste of soup stock in China and Western countries. Dashi is used to add umami to almost all boiled dishes and soups, just as bouillon is used in Western or Chinese cooking. Lacking meat, which is a rich source of umami, the Japanese derived umami from dried fish, seaweed, and vegetables.

Kyoto is one of the most historical cities in Japan. It was the capital of Japan for about a thousand years since 794 when the Heian era began. The long history of being the center of Japan has affected the current style of Kyoto cuisine. Zen monks, who had played an important role in the development of Japanese cuisine from the Muromachi period (1333-1573), had particular problems making dashi. Because of their strict vegetarian dishes, monks were not allowed to eat dashi made from fish. In these vegetarian dishes, dried kombu was most favored by the common people of Japan.

Kombu

Kombu is a general term for brown algae. There are various species of algae. Among them, those most commonly utilized as dashi materials are makombu, rishiri-kombu, rausu-kombu and hidaka-kombu which are only harvested around Hokkaido island in Japan. Kombu, growing 3-10 meters long in two years on the coasts of Hokkaido, is harvested and sun dried on the beach and shipped. Only Kombu which has matured for two years is used for dashi (kombu broth) for cooking, because one-year-old kombu is called 'water kombu' since it does not contain the rich components needed for a good flavour. From the Muromachi period, kombu was harvested along the coast of Hokkaido, and shipped to Kyoto, the capital of Japan, and then to Osaka, the center of commerce. The distance from

Hokkaido to Kyoto or Osaka is more than 1200 km. A route designed for the transportation of kombu from Hokkaido to other parts of Japan is called the 'Kombu road'. This fact shows how important kombu was for people living in Kyoto and Osaka. It is interesting to note that people living in Hokkaido have no tradition of using kombu as a source of dashi.

Now, from July to September, live kombu is harvested in special boats and brought to the shore where it is dried, first in the sun, and then by hot-air fans in special drying chambers. The dried kombu is then allowed to mature for two years. Rich in glutamate, the kombu is sold in markets to be used as an important raw material for preparing 'dashi'.

Dried bonito (katsuobushi)

In ancient Japan, concentrated extracts were called 'irori' paste, a concentrated bonito soup produced during the making of dried bonito, 'katsuobushi'. Katsuobushi is the traditional material used for making Japanese soup stock. According to Japanese historical records, the earliest mention of something similar to dashi appears in the Laws and Regulations, written in the late Nara period (710-794). This reference, written in Chinese characters is read as 'katsuo-irori', meaning bonito broth. This concentrated paste is very rich in the umami taste imparted by inosinate. However, katusobushi which is used to make modern soup stock, had not been created at that time. Katsuobushi was invented some time during the Edo period (1603-1867). The basic recipe for making dried bonito is as follows: The bonito is boiled, dried for a long time, smoked, and then fermented with fungi. The irori paste is the concentrate of the brew remaining after boiling the bonito in the above process. Unlike dried bonito, irori paste has disappeared from mainstream Japanese cuisine. Today, the products most similar to the ancient irori paste come from Makurazaki, in the south of Kyushu. Dried bonito is also made in the Maldives. There, bonito fillet is simply boiled and dried to make a product known as 'Maldive fish'. Ibn Battutah, a 14th century traveler, wrote that large numbers of Maldive fish were being exported from the Maldives to other countries. The product is still consumed locally and is also exported to Sri Lanka. A concentrated paste of the bonito soup derived from the first stage of making maldive fish is called 'rihakuru'. Rihakuru is used as a seasoning. In both Japan and the Maldives, the same methods are used to make dried bonito, and the concentrated bonito soup is used to add the richness of umami to various dishes. In the Maldives, concentrated bonito paste is normally consumed in much the same manner as in 12th century Japan; the paste is used as seasoning for boiled fish.

Dashi, the most simple umami soup

Preparing Kombu dashi, a pure umami soup, is very simple. Cut a dried kombu sheet (usually about 15-20 cm wide) into about 20cm. Heat the kombu and 1 litre of water in a large saucepan over a medium heat. Just before the water boils, take out the kombu. Over heating or long boiling causes scum to form.

One famous Japanese chef, who actively introduced fusion style Japanese cuisine all over the world, told us his unique experience. A French chef, who was cooking with him had boasted that it took a week to prepare top quality stock or bouillon for French sauces, while Japanese dashi could be quickly prepared in ten minutes. The Japanese chef explained that a long, labor-intensive process was required to produce the kombu and dried bonito flakes that are the essence of dashi. Kombu is cultivated for two years before being carefully sun dried. More than six months are needed to make the dried flakes from fresh bonito. Once the French chef learnt the secret of Japanese dashi, he went quiet.

Soy sauce

Soy sauce is an indispensable element of Japanese cooking, used in simmering, grilling, frying, dressing etc. It is obtained through the biochemical breakdown of soybeans and wheat components in the presence of salt, and by the actions of microorganisms added in the form of koji. Soybean components contribute to its umami and unique reddish hues. It is said that soy sauce was first commercially produced in 1290 in a town

called Yuasa near Osaka, the commercial center of Japan. In the middle of the seventeenth century, the Dutch from Nagasaki exported soy sauce, from one of the most westerly cities of Japan. At that time, Japan was following a policy of national isolation and the government prohibited foreign intercourse or trade. Only in Nagasaki, the prohibition was relaxed slightly and trade in a few limited items continued. Soy sauce was one of a few export items, which the Dutch shipped to Europe, especially France. There, presumably, Japanese soy sauce was used as a 'secret flavor' in the feasts prepared in the kitchens of the Court.

Culinary art and science

Umami is a new word, but an old taste. Most food materials, either animal or vegetable, contain amino acids and nucleic acids, and all civilizations have appreciated the taste. However, basic theory of taste elements never seemed to be related to umami. For more than 2000 years, from Aristole to Henning, many theories have been presented on the basic tastes. The Japanese had a question about the unique, subtle but important taste element in dashi, it is not sweet, sour, salty, or bitter. The question was raised by Prof. Kikunae Ikeda who grew up in Kyoto, a historically important place in the forming of the foundations of Japanese cuisine. As previously explained, Prof. Ikeda found that glutamate was the major taste element making up the taste of dashi using kombu. In his report at the 8th International Congress of Applied Chemistry, 1912, Ikeda appealed at length to the scientists who were not interested in the taste. He aroused the attention of his audience stating that if they carefully tasted asparagus, tomatoes, cheese, or meat, they would notice, in the complicated taste of those foods, a common but quite unique taste that was entirely different from the four other tastes. He emphasized that as sweet is expressed as the taste of sugar, umami can be expressed as the taste of glutamate. Four years after Ikeda's report, Kodama found that inosinate was responsible for the umami taste in katsuobushi. In 1960, guanylate was found to be the substance of umami in shiitake mushrooms by Dr. Kuninaka. He also found that there was a great synergism between glutamate and inosinate or guanylate.

The umami taste, of course, is not limited to Japan and Asia. Bouillon, soup stocks and many basic sauces of French cooking are the culmination of efforts to draw out umami and impart it to various dishes. How did the Japanese identify the umami taste? There are two conceivable ways. One relates to the use of oils and animal fats in Western countries, while

neither were used in traditional Japanese cuisine. The second reason is cultural. Although the West has familiar substances exhibiting the epitome of each taste, such as sugar for sweet and salt for salty, no such substance exists for umami. In Japan, this role has been played by dashi.

In recent years, many Japanese chefs have been working globally. They export not only culinary art but also philosophy worldwide. Many chefs in the world are interested in the culinary art of Japanese cuisine. As scientific evidence shows, umami is an independent taste element along with the other four; sweet, sour, salty and bitter, and chefs are trying to know and explain the umami taste in their cooking. Cooking is an art. The fusion of traditional Japanese and Western style dishes is not only an art expressed through careful presentation on the plate, but also through the gustatory sensation of umami and other tastes.

Umami has become a global word. Enjoy the umami taste in your cooking!

Umami in Western Cuisine (by Elizabeth Rozin)

Central to the culinary endeavor in humans everywhere is the production and experience of flavor. No matter where they live or the specific characteristics of their history and culture, people all over the world, and indeed throughout history, have expended tremendous energy, time, and ingenuity in achieving what they regard as a good and appropriate flavor for the food they consume. The details of the enterprise vary, from area to area and group to group, but the need appears to be compelling and universal.

The flavor phenomenon

The flavor of food is a complex phenomenon that occurs on many different levels. There is the flavor of the food substance itself, the subtle brininess of an oyster, for example, or the tangy sweetness of ripe pineapple. Then there is the flavor additionally provided by the cooking or preservative techniques employed: boiled beef tastes very different from grilled beef, even when no other ingredients have been added; a raisin dried in the sun has a flavor unlike the original grape from which it is made, as well as a dissimilar texture and appearance. From most cultures, the flavor inherent in the foodstuffs and the flavor produced by various processing techniques are an essential part of the flavor experience, but they are by no means the whole story.

It is a characteristic practice of people everywhere to further enhance their food by adding ingredients that frequently seem to have no other function than to heighten, transform or improve the flavor. These seasoning ingredients can be added to the food before or during the cooking process, or added to cooked food at the end as an accompaniment or condiment. They may consist of simple unprocessed substances, such as freshly chopped herbs or lemon juice, or complex manufactured compounds such as soy sauce or mustard. Whatever their makeup and method of application, however, they seem to operate similarly in a variety of diverse cultures throughout the world.

When we look at the flavoring practices of culinary traditions almost everywhere, we can see a clear tendency to select a limited number of seasoning substances and to use those ingredients constantly and pervasively in combination. These seasoning compounds, which I call 'Flavor Principles', provide powerful and characteristic flavor profiles that are familiar and pleasing to those within the culture, recognizable and replicable to those from without. Think, for example, of two widely divergent cuisines, Greek and Indonesian, which both grill chunks of lamb over charcoal. The Greek souvlaki is characteristically flavored with lemon and oregano, while the

Indonesian satay is typically seasoned with a sweet and spicy blend of soy sauce, coconut, chili pepper, and ground peanuts. The same basic food and cooking techniques here result in two wholly different dishes whose distinctiveness resides in the characteristic flavoring compounds. Similarly, we can contemplate two varieties of boiled wheat-flour noodles, one Chinese, the other southern Italian. The Chinese version is likely to have a sauce based on soy sauce, ginger root, and sesame oil, while the Neapolitan is almost certain to feature a sauce made from olive oil, garlic, tomatoes, and basil. There is no confusing the two dishes, for the sensory experience each offers by way of flavoring ingredients is characteristic and unique.

Categories of flavor principles

The component ingredients of ethnic flavor principles can be classified in various categories. The first of these is that of fats or oils, which are among the most effective of flavoring agents because they both carry their own unique flavors and are also powerful conveyors of other flavors. The distinctive taste of different meats, for example, comes from the surrounding and marbled fat within the muscle tissue. Oils of vegetable origin (sesame, olive, peanut, etc.) and fats of animal origin (lard, chicken or bacon fat, meat drippings, butter, etc.) can also be further processed to provide additional desirable flavor; the toasting of sesame seeds to obtain a fragrant flavorful oil; the cooking and clarifying of butter to produce the nutty-flavored Indian ghee.

A second category of flavoring substances comprises liquids, semi-liquids, and concentrated pastes, typically used in soups, stews, and sauces. These products are of both animal and vegetable origin and can be made from fresh or cultured (fermented) substances. Fresh animal-based liquids include meat, poultry, fish or seafood stocks, milk and cream. Cultured animal-based liquids include fermented fish sauce and dairy products such as sour cream, yogurt, and cheese. Familiar fresh vegetable-based liquids are crushed tomatoes, coconut milk, and a variety of vegetable juices and infusions. Cultured or fermented vegetable liquids include such widely used products as wine and vinegar, beer, soy sauce and bean pastes, and sauerkraut juice. Every one of these products offers a unique and distinctive flavoring element to the food in which or with which it is prepared and served.

A third category involves a wide variety of ingredients typically added in relatively small amounts, specifically for their seasoning properties, and occurring in both fresh and processed forms. They include aromatics such as onion, scallion, leek, garlic, shallot, sweet peppers, carrot, celery, ginger root, lemon grass, etc. Also included are the pungent or irritant ingredients— chili peppers, black pepper, horseradish, and mustard. Widely used are a large array of fresh green herbs such as parsley, dill, basil, mint, and cilantro, and an impressive assortment of spices provided by bark, leaves, berries, and seeds. Also in this category are acidic ingredients such as lemon, lime, and tamarind, and flavored sweeteners such as honey, maple syrup, fruit juices and concentrates.

The many substances used to flavor food frequently serve multiple or overlapping culinary functions; wine, for example, may be used as the primary liquid in a dish, but it also contributes an acidic note that might be inappropriate if provided by lime juice or yogurt; sesame oil delivers its characteristic nutty flavor and aroma to food while providing at the same time a pleasing richness and unctuous mouth-feel. The interaction between food and flavor, ingredient and technique, is complex and many-layered, yet it has evolved with an astonishing regularity throughout the human culinary enterprise.

When we acknowledge the extent and persistence of flavoring practices through the centuries and across cultures, we understand that flavor is a

central and crucial part of the food experience. Whatever other vital functions our need and ability to cook may serve—increasing the nutritional value of foods, improving digestibility, preventing spoilage, eliminating dangerous or unpleasant elements—the application or production of appropriate and pleasing flavor is primary in our understanding of the food we eat and in our understanding of who we are.

The function of flavor

First, flavor provides a sensory label for our food that enables us to identify ourselves as members of a culture or group: the constant use of onions, lard, paprika, and sour cream makes Hungarian food Hungarian, and not Malaysian or Portuguese; the flavoring of soup with dried bonito, kelp, and red bean paste labels that food as Japanese and no other. This sensory labeling is a process that almost certainly begins in utero and is subsequently expressed in the distinctive flavor and aroma of the mother's milk. Consistently recurring flavor defines our food and identifies it as familiar, appropriate, good and safe.

Second, flavor serves to enhance the appeal of bland or boring foods.

Because of geographic, economic, or religious constraints, many people throughout the world are limited to diets composed mainly of starchy, mealy, bland vegetable foods. The consumption of grains, roots, tubers, legumes, and starchy fruits may be required in relatively large amounts in order to satisfy minimal nutritional requirements, and these foods can become boring and unpalatable unless they are enhanced with flavoring ingredients that make the eating experience more varied and more interesting. Indeed, there seems to be a clear correlation between high vegetable or starch-based diets and strong, salient seasoning practices; in these traditions, the heavy seasoning looks very much like a need or substitute for meat or meatiness.

Gustatory satisfaction

Underlying this quest for added, improved, or enhanced flavor is the apparently universal human desire to find gustatory satisfaction, to experience from food a pleasure and gratification that transcends the merely nutritional.

All people, all cuisines manifest this inclination, although they accomplish it in different ways and from a wide variety of different ingredients. The goal of the behavior seems remarkably parallel: the production of mouth-filling flavor that is variously described as 'full', 'rich', 'meaty', 'savory', 'round'. One seasoning, salt is clearly universal, but there may well be other less apparent substances that operate to provide gustatory satisfaction in cultures worldwide. These are the glutamates; naturally occurring substances that appear to intensify or enhance flavor, producing a pleasurable and satisfying taste called umami.

Umami in Asian cuisine

Umami, which is commonly translated as 'savoriness' or 'deliciousness', was first defined and described with reference to Asian, and particularly Japanese cuisine, where it is found in such typical seasonings as soy sauce, bean paste, dried fish, kelp, a variety of seafood and shiitake mushrooms. Perhaps because of its early association with these Asian-specific ingredients, it has not been extensively investigated in the culinary traditions of the West. A closer look reveals, however, that umami is a profound and significant element in both traditional and contemporary western flavoring practices.

Meat in Western cuisine

Meat is a rich source of Glutamic acid, and is fundamental to the production of flavor in western tradition. Beef and pork are primary meats used for this purpose. The great nineteenth century French chef Carême declared that 'beef is the soul of cooking'; by this he meant that the flesh, fat, and bones of beef, boiled with vegetables and aromatics, seasoned, strained and clarified, formed the essential basis of the great classic sauces, stocks, and soups. Called 'broth' or 'bouillon' (from the French word 'bouilli', boiled), these savory, glutamate-rich, meaty liquids are frequently cooked down and reduced into concentrated pastes or jellies that are then added in small quantities to soups and sauces as potent flavor enrichers; typical examples of such products are the French 'glace de viande', a concentrated essence of beef, and the English, Canadian, and Australian Bovril, a commercially bottled glutamate-enhanced beef concentrate. The English also traditionally consumed a less complex strained meaty liquid called beef tea, prepared from shaved lean beef steeped in hot water, and taken primarily as a curative or restorative tonic.

At the end of the nineteenth century, a Swiss manufacturer developed concentrated bouillon for commercial purposes, and in recent decades there has been a proliferation of these 'instant' powders, pastes, and bouillon cubes. Made primarily of beef but increasingly of chicken as well, they offer a convenient, inexpensive source of meaty flavor and flavor enhancement. Less fresh-tasting and complex than a homemade stock or concentrate prepared from choice ingredients, they nonetheless provide a quick and easy way to 'beef up' the flavor of many liquid-based dishes.

Pork, like beef and other meats, is a generous source of Glutamic acid. Unlike beef, however, its use as a flavoring agent in western tradition occurs largely as a cured product—dried, salted, smoked, and aged. The curing process liberates more of the Glutamic acid content of the meat, contributing to a richer, fuller flavor, the taste of umami. Except for Jews and Muslims, whose religions forbid the consumption of pork, many western cuisines have exploited cured pork to provide a rich savory flavor for their food.

There has developed from ancient times in the West an extensive repertoire of cured pork products such as ham, bacon, salt pork, smoked ham hocks and neck bones, and a great variety of sausages made from ground or chopped pork that is additionally spiced and seasoned, then cured. Each cuisine or region produces its own characteristic variety; Spanish chorizo, Italian pepperoni, Polish kielbasa, and German frankfurters are but a few of the vast assortment of cured sausages that are typically used to add flavor and richness to many prepared foods. Such classic regional French dishes as the Alsatian choucroute garni (dressed-up sauerkraut) and the southwestern cassoulet derive their hearty savor from a wide variety of cured pork products.

The cured pork tradition traveled from Europe to the Americas, where it was enthusiastically adopted by both Native Americans and later immigrant groups. Smoked and salted pork give their full distinctive flavor to all sorts of popular staple foods — potatoes, rice, vegetables, beans, and legumes — in a number of traditional soups, stews, gravies, and sauces. They appear in such ethnically diverse dishes as New England Clam Chowder with salt pork, Southern Cooked Collard Greens with smoked ham hocks, German-style Potato Salad with bacon, Creole Jambalaya, rice with spicy sausage, and Cuban Black Beans with ham. Furthermore, the wide popularity of cold sliced luncheon meat — ham, salami, bologna, etc. — another legacy from Europe, is more evidence of the powerful appeal of cured pork

products to provide a rich and savory flavor to sandwiches and other rolled or layered bread and pasta constructions. The specific seasonings may vary from product to product and dish to dish, but the pleasing full umami taste underlies them all.

Dairy products in Western cuisine

Along with the strong focus on meat in much of western culinary tradition, there is an intensive corollary use of dairy products. These products, both fresh and cultured, come primarily from cow's milk and to a lesser extent from sheep's or goat's milk, all of which contain plentiful amounts of Glutamic acid (although cow's milk is by far the richest source). When the milk is cultured with enzymes, molds, or bacilli and aged or cured to produce cheese, further Glutamic acid is liberated, with a corresponding boost in flavor. It is no coincidence, then, that the harder or more aged the cheese, the more it is used for its seasoning properties, a practice common in many western cuisines. Such familiar cheeses as the Italian parmesan and Romano, the French and Swiss Emmental and Gruyère, English and American cheddar and cheddar-types, are frequently used to provide savory toppings for cooked food, or stirred into sauces to add additional depths of savory flavor. Other mold-cured varieties such as Roquefort, made from sheep's milk, and the blue cheese-types, made from cow's milk, lend their distinctive glutamate-rich flavors to spreads, sauces, and salad dressings.

Additional cultured dairy products, such as yogurt and sour cream, also play a major role in the flavoring practices of many western cuisines. They are a less concentrated source of glutamate than aged cheese and their flavor is further qualified by the unique tang of the lactic acid that is a result of the culturing process. They are nonetheless an ancient and traditional member of the umami family, valued as both food and flavor in central

Europe, Greece, the Balkans, and the Middle East, used in sauces, soups, salads, and condiments.

Fish in Western cuisine

The use of dried and fermented fish and seafood products is much less pervasive in western tradition than in Asian cuisines, but it is by no means absent. Much of the food of ancient Rome was routinely seasoned with a sauce called 'garum' or 'liquamen', which was made from salted fish, fermented and strained, and was very likely similar to the popular fish sauces of Southeast Asia. The Roman fish sauce tradition died out (along with the Roman Empire), but was replaced in large part by salted anchovies, heavily utilized in southern Italy, Sicily, and southern France as a flavor enhancing ingredient in sauces for meat, vegetables, and pasta and as a savory addition to pizza, salads, and hors d'oeuvre. Now widely available, packed

whole in olive oil or processed into tubes of creamy paste, salted anchovies are used throughout western Europe and America to add a delicious concentrated fishy glutamate – rich flavor to sauces, spreads, and salad dressings. They are a constant component of a number of traditional English seasoning and condiment sauces, such as Worcestershire and steak sauces, and give their characteristic flavor to the popular Caesar Salad. Blended with softened butter, salted anchovies provide a savory spread for bread, grilled meats, and vegetables.

Other examples of the western use of fish and seafood products for flavor are the dried shrimp frequently found in some of the soups, stews, and mixed rice dishes of Central and South America, especially Brazil and the Caribbean. This practice probably derives not from Europe but from sub-Saharan Africa, where dried fish and seafood are commonly added to stews and sauces to provide a fuller, richer flavor. Finally, there are the rich savory fish and seafood soups that are so typically prepared throughout the Mediterranean, the Caribbean, and the American Gulf states. In dishes like the French bouillabaisse, the Spanish Sopa de mariscos, and the New Orleans Gumbo, a wide variety of fresh fish and shellfish, including the flesh, bones, and shells, are simmered with herbs and aromatics to make savory, intensely flavored broths to which more seafood may be added for a full and satisfying dish. These strained broths, with their flavorful load of sea-based glutamates, are probably the closest western equivalent to the traditional Japanese dashi.

Two other traditions should be noted, though both are somewhat limited in their availability and/or appeal. The polar Eskimo people traditionally fermented a small portion of their harvest of fish; the fish was consumed partially frozen, and the riper and more fully flavored it became, the more it was esteemed as a special delicacy. Small wonder, that in the frozen wastes of the Arctic, the rich flavor of fermented fish gives pleasurable savor to a diet and a culinary practice severely constrained by a harsh and difficult climate. Another delicacy is caviar, the salted roe of several varieties of sturgeon; it is a costly and prestigious food in much of the West, eaten in small quantities on special occasions. I have not been able to ascertain the glutamate content of caviar, but it likely contains a generous supply.

The tomato as an umami source

Of the many plant foods that provide umami in western tradition, the tomato is foremost. It is, interestingly, a relative newcomer on the world stage, for it was native to the Americas and unknown anywhere in Europe, Asia, or Africa until after the Spanish conquest of Mexico early in the sixteenth century. Since that time it has come to play a major role in the cuisines of the Mediterranean, the Balkans, the Middle East, and contemporary America, used fresh in salads, relishes, and sandwiches, and cooked into a wide variety of robust sauces, soups, and condiments. It is available in a remarkable assortment of processed forms: whole, chopped, strained, in purees, sauces, and concentrated pastes, as a savory beverage or vegetable 'cocktail'.

The attractive full, round flavor of tomatoes comes from a heavy load of glutamates, and the 'meaty' flavor is reinforced by the tomato's unique crimson color, the color of blood, the very essence of animal life. In Orthodox Judaism, blood is a substance sacred to the Lord and may not be consumed under any circumstances. It was for this reason, apparently, that the tomato, even though a plant food, was initially rejected by certain orthodox Jews of Eastern Europe. For many other people, however, these qualities are very appealing, and tomatoes in a variety of forms are appreciated for both their full flavor and color-enhancing capacities. In many western cuisines a spoonful or two of concentrated tomato paste is frequently added to a soup or a stew to give enhanced flavor, body, and color.

It is not surprising, then, that some of the West's most popular foods contain tomatoes as a primary ingredient – tacos and salsa, spaghetti with tomato sauce, pizza, burgers and French fries garnished with ketchup. Indeed, ketchup, the most familiar and traditional of American condiments, illustrates in its own history the different ways umami is produced and expressed in a number of ethnic cuisines. Ketchup originated in Southeast Asia; its name derives from 'kecap', the Indonesian term for soy sauce. In the seventeenth century, merchants and sailors of the British East India Company brought soy sauce back to England, where it was refashioned as a condimental sauce based on locally available ingredients such as walnuts and mushrooms. The tradition traveled to America with English settlers; in the New World the sauce underwent another transformation, this time with the indigenous tomato, which gave it its now familiar flavor and vibrant color. (Incidentally, tomato ketchup is sometimes referred to as tomato soy in England.) And so the umami theme remains constant, even though the medium through which it is expressed may vary from culture to culture, beginning in Asia with fermented soy beans, migrating through

English walnuts and mushrooms, emerging triumphant with tomatoes in America, ketchup is evidence of the worldwide inclination to exploit glutamate-rich foods for savory seasonings and condiments.

The mushroom as an umami source

Mushrooms are another plant food widely appreciated in the West for the deep earthy flavors they contribute to sauces and gravies, stews and ragouts. The glutamate content of mushrooms varies from type to type, but most varieties contain plentiful amounts. Used both fresh and dried, they add rich flavor and interesting texture to many characteristic dishes in Italy and

France, and especially in the central and eastern European cuisines of Hungary and Poland. Frequently they combine with and synergistically enhance other glutamate-rich foods such as meat, tomatoes, and dairy products. Some varieties, like the highly prized porcini and

morels, are dried to produce an even more intensely flavorful product; the liquid in which they are rehydrated is typically strained and added to the pot to enhance the final flavor of the dish.

The shiitake mushroom, for centuries an esteemed ingredient in the Asian repertoire, with the highest glutamate content of all mushrooms, has only recently been introduced to the West. In America it has become very popular and is now widely available, valued for its exceptionally rich flavor, and used not only in Asian-style dishes, but in a wide range of preparations.

Other glutamate rich products

Other seasoning products fashioned from plant substances rich in glutamates include a number of concentrated extracts or pastes made from malt or yeast; they are developed primarily in the English tradition and are used to boost the flavor of sauces, gravies, and condiments. In Australia, yeast extracts called 'Vegemite' or 'Marmite' are spread on buttered bread to make a savory sandwich commonly prepared for children. In some areas of the Caribbean, particularly those with a history of English influence, these extracts turn up as convenient, inexpensive flavor enhancers for soups and sauces.

To sum up

This brief review makes clear that the umami tradition in the West differs in some significant ways from that of the East. In terms of ingredients, umami in most Asian cuisines is derived from fermented soy beans, prepared whole, in sauces, and in concentrated pastes from an impressive assortment of dried and/or fermented fish and seafood products; and from such characteristic ingredients as shiitake mushrooms and seaweed. In the West, umami from ancient times has been heavily associated with meat, primarily beef and cured pork, and a wide range of fresh and cultured dairy products, which have never been a significant part of the Southeast Asian tradition. Plant sources vary as well, with the widely popular tomato replacing the Asian soy bean as a sauce vehicle and flavor-enhancing additive.

Differences in flavor production techniques

There are also differences between East and West in the techniques of flavor production. Asian tradition has long focused on fermentation as a central and favored technique, with particular reference to soy beans and a variety of fish and seafood. Western tradition, on the other hand, relies more heavily on the techniques of extraction, reduction, and concentration to obtain its familiar and pleasing umami preparations. This basic difference in culinary practice is no doubt to do with the nature and composition of the ingredients available for processing, although it is not entirely clear whether it is the ingredients or the techniques that take precedence in the formation of any tradition. Whatever the origins, the characteristic products resulting from the combination of ingredient and technique are encoded and perpetuated in cultural tradition.

Fats, oils and umami

Finally, there is in the West a powerful association of umami foods with fats and oils. This is at least in part a function of the age-old western taste for meat and dairy products, with their natural endowment of animal fat, although it is useful to remember that the Glutamic acid that provides the umami taste, resides in the muscle tissue of the meat, while the characteristic flavor is carried through the fat. However, the taste for fat is not limited to its association with meat; it extends to other umami foods as well. Salted anchovies are almost always preserved in olive oil, mixed or cooked with olive oil in the Mediterranean and with butter in other areas

of Western and Northern Europe. The tomato, so enthusiastically adopted from its original Mexican homeland, is almost always prepared as a fresh vegetable with oil-based salad dressings, or cooked with olive oil into rich savory sauces, and frequently enhanced with a variety of cheeses. Fresh mushrooms are usually sautéed in some kind of fat or oil before they are served or added to other foods, and both fresh and dried mushrooms are commonly used in conjunction with fatty rich cream, sour cream, and cheese sauces. The unique relationship between umami foods and fat in western culinary tradition is clear and characteristic, and is certainly a subject for further investigation.

Differences and similarities

Despite these obvious differences between East and West in terms of ingredients and techniques, of emphasis and style, there is a remarkable similarity in structure and motivation. The Southeast Asian cuisines of Thailand, Vietnam, Burma and the Philippines, for example, are all based on a glutamate-rich seasoning agent – fermented fish sauce – but each cuisine individualizes itself with the addition of certain characteristic flavoring ingredients. Similarly, the cuisines of the Mediterranean, the Balkans, and the Middle East make heavy use of the glutamate-rich tomato as a savory base for much cooked food, but again, each tradition characterizes its flavor with separate sets of seasoning ingredients, and although there is frequent overlap between these neighboring cuisines, their seasoning profiles remain distinctive and recognizable.

Underlying all of these culturally individualized flavor principles is a basic umami substance, operating as what seems to be a king of universal medium for the experience of gustatory satisfaction. The umami medium itself varies, as we have seen, from the soybean and seafood products of Asia to the tomato sauces of the Americas and the Mediterranean to the concentrated meat stocks and dairy products of Europe, but the umami taste is common to them all. However we choose to describe the experience it offers – 'savory', 'rich', 'brothy', 'tasty', 'chickeny', 'delicious', 'meaty' - we all seem to want it and enjoy it as a fundamental part of what makes our food taste good. However differently we may define and produce it, we appear to experience it in the same way and to value it for the same reasons.

Umami and its central role

Some western cooks and consumers have resisted the use of monosodium glutamate as a refined flavor-enhancing additive, perceiving it as somehow unnatural or even dangerous, yet these same people have no hesitation in using concentrated bouillon cubes and powders to create soups and sauces, or in adding a good shot of Worcestershire sauce, ketchup or steak sauce to boost the flavor of their food. They would not wish to cook up a potful of beans without adding a fat smoked ham hock for flavor, or eat a plateful of spaghetti without a rich hearty tomato sauce liberally sprinkled with grated parmesan cheese. The beloved American cheeseburger is a

layered construction of umami foods, from the ground beef patty to the cheese to the ketchup; a slice of pizza offers bits of sausage or anchovy, cheese, and savory tomato sauce in every delicious bite. These popular foods provide other appealing features, of course: plenty of fat and salt, textural variety, attractive color and design, but underlying all the sensory experiences and common to all these products are the glutamates, mouth-filling and satisfying.

From the great classic sauces of French haute cuisine to the robust, highly seasoned peasant dishes of the Mediterranean and the Balkans, from the spicy eclectic blends of the Caribbean to the hearty, plain 'meat and potatoes' preference of rural Midwestern America, umami plays a central and crucial role. Although it was first identified and described with specific reference to Asian foods, it has clearly always been, and will certainly continue to be, a fundamental feature of western cuisine.

Elizabeth Rozin Biography

PUBLICATIONS

Books:

Crossroads Cooking, Viking, NY, 1999

The Universal Kitchen, Viking Penguin, NY, 1996.

The Primal Cheeseburger, Viking Penguin, NY, 1994.

Blue Corn and Chocolate, Alfred A. Knopf, NY, Judith Jones, ed. 1992

Ethnic Cuisine: The Flavor Principle Cookbook, Stephen Greene Press, 1983

Reprinted in paperback, 1985, Re-issue by Viking Penguin, 1992

The Flavor Principle Cookbook, Hawthorn, NY, 1973

Articles:

"The Role of Flavor in the Meal and the Culture" Dimentions of the Meal, H. Meiselaman, ed. Aspen Pbulishers, 2000.

"Saveurs Pour Tous". Milles et Une Bouches, dirige par Bessis, S. Autrement, Paris, 1995.

"The Great Ketchup-Salsa Debate". Icarus, Vol. 9, January, 1993.

"Aesthetics and Cuisine: Mine Over Matter". Beauty and the Brain, I. Rentschler, B. Herzberger, and D. Epstein, eds. Burkhauser-Verlag, 1988.

"Ketchup and the Collective Unconscious", Journal of Gastronomy, 1988.

"Traditional Recipes of Laos by Phia Sing" (Review). Appetite, 1982.

"The Structure of Cuisine". The Psychobiology of Human Food Selection, L.M. Barker, ed. AVI, 1982.

"Culinary Themes and Variations". Natural History, 1981 (with Paul Rozin).

"Culinary Themes and Variations". The Professional Nutritionist, 1981.

TEACHING EXPERIENCE

University of Pennsylvania, College of General Studies, Philadelphia, PA, 1979-1987.

• Culture and Cuisine: Three Food Systems - Chinese, Hindu, and Orthodox Jewish

• Fascinating Foods: Seasonings, Dairy Products and Chocolate

• International Flavors in University City

• Great American Cuisine

• The Culinary Enterprise

• Appetites and Aversions

Cottonwood Gulch Foundation, Thoreau, NM 1984 and 1991

• Pre-Columbian Cuisine

INVITED ADDRESSES AND MEDIA APPEARANCES

"Native American Foods". Native American Day, University of Pennsylvania Museum. Philadelphia, PA, September, 1992 & 1995.

"Chocolate and Chile". The Maya Society, University of Pennsylvania Museum. April, 1994.

"Preserved Fish as Seasoning". Symposium on Fish, Shellfish, and Fisheries in America. National Museum of American History, Smithsonian Institution, Washington, D.C., October, 1994.

"Historic Roots of Fusion Cuisine". Panelist. Summit in the Sun. South Florida Chapter, American Institute of Wine and Food. Miami, FL, October, 1994.

"Food and Flavor: From the Nose to the Table". (Children's Workshop). Conference on Feeding Our Future. American Institute of Wine and Food. Monterey, CA, March, 1994.

"From Ketchup to salsa - Defining American Taste: Ohio Chapter of Institute of Food Technologists. Cincinnati, OH, March, 1994.

"In Pursuit of the Hot Tomato". U.S. Army Research & Development Conference on Foods Preservation 2000. Natick, MA., November, 1993.

"A Passion for Chocolate". Young Audiences of Indiana Chocolate Festival. Indianapolis, IN, October, 1993.

"Ethnic Flavors: Seasoning for Health". Philadelphia Nutrition Society, Monell Center for the Chemical Senses. Philadelphia, PA, April, 1993.

"Chocolate - A History". Panel Leader. Conference on Foods of the Americas. American Institute of Wine and Food. Washington, D.C., March, 1993.

"Historical Storytelling-The Tomato". Conference on Foods of the Americas. American Institute of Wine and Food. Washington, D.C., March 1993.

"Blue Corn and Chocolate-from the New World to the Old". Philadelphia Maritime Museum. Philadelphia, PA, October, 1992.

"Peanuts-America's Gift to the World". Peanut Advisory Board. Athens, GA, September, 1992.

"New World Foods and American Cuisine". Resident Associates Program, Smithsonian Institution. July, 1992.

"Food and Flavor". Baltimore-Washington Chapter, Institute of Food Technologists. Baltimore, May, 1992.

"A New World of Food-Implications for Health and Nutrition". Pennsylvania Dietetic Association. Philadelphia, May, 1992.

"The Book and the Cook". Serrano Restaurant, Philadelphia, PA, 1988, 1989, 1992.

"Cultural, Biological and Ecological Basis of Cuisine: a seminar in the Biological Basis of Behavior". University of Pennsylvania, Philadelphia, PA, 1987.

"The Potato-A Bumpy History". New York Chapter, American Institute of Wine and Food. New York, 1990.

"Three Culinary information features on "Spotlight", WPBS-TV. Philadelphia, PA, 1986.

"Food for Thought" (BBC Natural History program on food. Interviewee and Consultant, 1986.

"From Calories to Cuisine". American Psychological Association. Toronto, Ontario, 1984.

Basic Information about Umami

Natural occurrence

Glutamate is naturally present in most foods, such as meat, poultry, seafood and vegetables. Two kinds of nucleotides that contribute most to the umami taste, inosinate and guanylate, are also present in many foods. Inosinate is found primarily in meat, whereas guanylate is more abundant in plants. Another nucleotide, adenylate, is abundant in fish and shellfish.

Umami substances In natural foods (mg/100g)

Glutamate		Inosinate	
Kombu	2240	Dried bonito	474
Parmegiano reggiano	1680	Tuna	286
Nori	1378	Chicken	283
Cured ham	337	Pork	260
Emmental Cheese	308	Beef	90
Tomato	246	Nori	9
Cheddar	182	Snow crab	5
Scallop	140	Sea urchin	2
Green asparagus	106		
Green pea	106	**Guanylate**	
Onion	51	Shiitake mushroom (dried)	150
Spinach	48	Morel (dried)	40
Green tea extract	32	Nori	13
Chicken	22	Fungi portini (dried)	10
Snow Crab	19	Oyster mushroom (dried)	10
Beef	10	Chicken	5
Potato	10	Beef	4
Pork	9	Snow crab	4
		Pork	2

Snow crab

Taste substances in snow crab can roughly be divided into five groups; amino acids, organic acids, nucleic acids, sugars and minerals. Though more than 40 taste components are found in snow crab meat, only seven taste substances shown in the table are essential in making up the taste of snow crab. Among these essential taste substances, glutamate and nucleotides contribute greatly to elevate the overall taste preference. The role of the seven taste substances in snow crab are shown in the table.

Essential taste components in snow crab
(mg/100ml)

Glycine	600
Alanine	200
Arginine	600
Glutamate	30
Inosinate	20
NaCl	500
K_2HPO_4	400

The tomato

Raymond Sakalov, a famous food journalist for The New York Times and The Wall Street Journal, said in his book 'Why we eat what we eat, how Columbus changed the way the world eats', that tomato focuses and improves recipes that were appealing before the tomato was available but that became extraordinarily attractive after it was added. Actually, the tomato from South America brought about a revolution in Italian dietary culture as well as many other countries in the world. Citric acid, glucose, potassium hydrogen phosphate, magnesium sulfate, calcium chloride, glutamate and aspartate reproduce the taste of tomato which is greatly affected by the ratio of glutamate to aspartate. The ratio and coexistence of both amino acids were the most important factors in reproducing the tomato taste. When no glutamate was added to the extract, the taste was similar to green tomato or citrus. It is difficult to perceive a clear umami taste in tomatoes, but it is one of the most important taste components in making up the taste along with sweet, sour and earthy tastes.

Parmesan cheese

Parmesan cheese is one of the world's most popular hard type cheeses. The Parmigiano reggiano, which has traditionally been produced in Parma, has a long history in Italy. The cheese was introduced in 'Decamerone' by Boccacio and was already being produced before the 10th century. More than two years are required for the maturation of the cheese. Grated Parmigiano reggiano is often used as a seasoning in Italian cuisine. The content of glutamate in the cheese is 1200-1600 mg/100g. It is historically true that people traditionally enjoy the taste of umami through the glutamate in Parmesan cheese. If you take a look at a big chunk of Parmesan cheese, you will find small white crystals. They are glutamate crystals that were formed during maturation.

Emmental cheese

Taste substances in Emmental cheese can be grouped into five taste categories as below:

Sweet: Proline, Alanine, Glycine, Threonine and Serine (All of these are amino acids)

Sour, salty and sweet: Lactic acid, succinic acid, Na, K. Mg. Ca, Cl, phophate and ammonia

Bitter: Valine, Leucine, Isoleucine, Phynylalanine, Tyrosine, Histidine, and Lysine

MSG-like or bouillon-like: glutamic acid

Burning: Tyramine and histamine

Swiss food scientists have reported that the most important taste characteristic of Emmental cheese is a sweet and bouillon-like flavor imparted by several amino acids including glutamate. The bouillon-like taste is the umami taste.

Umami and ripening

The ripening of vegetables generally makes them more flavorful. For example, flavor maturation in ripening tomatoes is related to the increase in natural content of free amino acids, namely glutamic acid and sugars. Though immature green tomatoes contain about 20mg/100g of free glutamate, full-ripened red tomatoes have more than eight times as much (260mg/100g). The tomato is used in various forms: canned, pure, paste, ketchup, chili sauce, etc. Discovery of the New World by Columbus in the 16th century brought us a variety of tomato products to add rich flavor to many different dishes.

During the ripening of cheese, proteins are broken down progressively into smaller polypeptides and individual amino acids. In particular, significant increases in leucine, glutamate, valine, lysine, phenylalanine and valine can be noted. Increases in these amino acids are generally recognized to be a reliable indicator of cheese ripening.

Large increases in free amino acid content also occur during the curing of ham and glutamate is the most abundant free amino acid found in the final product.

The flavor world of infants

Breastfeeding is a fundamental biological process that allows a mother to continue to nourish her infant after birth. Of the 20 free amino acids in human breast milk, glutamate is the most abundant, accounting for more than 50% of the total content. Its presence may influence taste acceptability to infants.

Neonatal human infants respond with a quiet and relaxed face when ingesting distilled or tap water. A sour taste always triggers nose wrinkling, lip pursing and some gaping, whereas bitter tasting solutions induce head shaking, frowning, tight closure of the eyes, depressed mouth corners, wide mouth opening and tongue protrusion, leading to wide gaping and sometimes spitting and drooling. In contrast, a sweet taste always induces eager sucking, smacking and licking movement.

Interestingly, an unseasoned vegetable broth causes facial displays similar to those induced by sour tasting liquid. However, umami seasoned vegetable broth triggers facial expressions very similar to those induced by a sweet taste. These results suggest that glutamate is a palatable taste stimulus for human infants. Because of its presence in breast milk, it might conceivably contribute to the taste acceptability of a soup that has the characteristic umami taste.

Synergistic effect

Although laymen may not understand the intricacies of synergism, they do know that a combination of kombu and bonito, or vegetables and meat makes for a tastier soup or sauce. Using such a combination is a developed way of creating the most flavorful dishes. The source of this multiplier effect is the combination of glutamate with nucleotides – the basis of umami. The sum of umami from a combination of glutamate and nucleotides can be more than the sum of its original parts. This is the synergistic effect of their interaction. It is evident that the magnitude of this interplay is unparalleled – up to eight times the properties of the ingredients. People traditionally utilized the combination before scientists unveiled this culinary secret.